G000045169

JOHN QUINCY

A Life from Beginning to End

Copyright © 2020 by Hourly History.

Table of Contents

Introduction

Born to John and Abigail Adams on July 11, 1767 in Massachusetts, this future president was himself the son of a president. His father John Adams would be elected as the second president of the United States in 1797, taking over the reins of the newly formed nation from George Washington. John Adams was the darling of the Federalist Party. Little did his son John Quincy know that he would one day be expected to follow in his father's footsteps. It was a path that had been cleared for him as early as 1777 when his father, who had been made a commissioner for an official delegation to France, had 10-year-old John Quincy Adams tag along.

It was just a couple of years into the American Revolutionary War, and the Americans were trying their best to convince France—the first country to recognize America's proclaimed independence—to remain supportive of the cause. It was a high stakes game of political brinkmanship at work, and a true sight to behold. Yet this was not the reason that little John Quincy was made to attend. He was summoned because his mother Abigail feared that father and son were drifting apart due to John Quincy's frequent business trips away from home. She insisted that the young boy go with his father so that the two could bond.

It wasn't exactly the best circumstances for a father and son outing in the midst of terrible trans-Atlantic conflict. In fact, before they even arrived at their destination, they were nearly overtaken by a hostile British craft. Luckily, the father and son duo safely reached French shores in the spring of 1778, and in the midst of all of this intrigue and international finagling, the seeds of John Quincy Adam's own political ambition would first take root.

Chapter One

A Child of the American Revolution

"The Declaration of Independence pronounced the irrevocable decree of political separation, between the United States and their people on the one part, and the British King, government, and nation on the other."

—John Quincy Adams

John Quincy Adams and his father arrived outside French shores on March 29, 1778, just in time to hear that the British had declared war on France. This was a great boon to the American revolutionaries because now they had a readymade ally in the form of France. It also made the efforts of John Quincy's father a whole lot easier since his most immediate objective had already been achieved.

John Quincy and his father disembarked from the docks on April 1, and a few days later on April 4, they were traveling by horse-drawn carriage to Paris. It was in Paris that Quincy's father would meet one of the most affable statesmen of the revolution—Benjamin Franklin. Franklin was a regular fixture of the Parisian social scene, and a true diplomatic force to be reckoned with. John Adams would end up tagging along with Franklin from one gala, party, and reception after another, where they endlessly stumped for support for the American cause. John Quincy, meanwhile, was deemed too young to attend these gatherings with his father and, as such, was usually left behind in the care of a few hired hands.

Eventually, John Quincy was placed into an exclusive French boarding school, keeping him preoccupied with his studies during the week before he caught up with his father on the weekend. It was the Sunday dinner in particular that was a major occasion for John Quincy; here, he would dine with his father and his fellow compatriot Benjamin Franklin. These were almost always extravagant gatherings in which Franklin sat at the table, with his circle of devotees crowding around him. At these meetings, the only thing more extravagant than the expensive wine and French food was the political discourse carried out at the table. Those in attendance would talk for hours on end about the latest political intrigue and happenings that were afoot in the world.

Along with this first-hand introduction to raw philosophy and political theory, John Quincy spent his days mastering the French language as well as Latin. Young John Quincy Adams became quite good at French, soon becoming fluent. Despite all of this rapid learning on the part of his son, the elder John Adams soon decided that their mission in France was an unnecessary one. Writing to Congress only a month or so after their arrival, John Adams indicated that he felt it would be best if Benjamin Franklin were designated as the sole American envoy to France. Feeling out of his element, Adams argued that Franklin could get the job done without his help.

With this early warning signal of correspondence fired across the Atlantic, it would take nearly a year for John Adams' handlers back in America to agree, recalling the diplomat back to the states in March of 1779. Finally, John Quincy was riding out of Paris with his father for the city of Nantes, near the Bay of Biscay, where they awaited a seafaring craft to take them back to America. Their vessel had been assigned elsewhere, however, and the pair were eventually led to the port city of Lorient, where after three whole months of waiting, they finally boarded a craft called the *Sensible* which would haul them back to America.

Abigail, for her part, was overwhelmed with joy to see the return of her husband and son. The local community by extension, couldn't have been happier as well. By popular demand, John Adams was elected to take part in a special convention tasked with fleshing out the nascent constitution for the state of Massachusetts.

Shortly after he finished this famous document of Massachusetts' statehood, Adams received word that he had been chosen to head a new diplomatic mission in France. Just a few months after his return, John Adams, with his precocious son in tow, was ready to leave for continental Europe once again.

Although John Quincy's mother was beside herself with frustration, writing to her husband at the time, "My habitation, how disconsolate it looks! My table, I sit down to it, but cannot swallow my food. Oh, why was I born with so much sensibility, and why, possessing it, have I so often been called to struggle with it? I wish to see you again." But regardless of how his mother felt at seeing her family

leave the country yet again, John Quincy Adams was more
than happy to pick up where he had left off.

Chapter Two

Adams' Mission in Europe and Russia

"We have no government armed with power capable of contending with human passions with unbridled by morality and religion. Our constitution was made for a moral and religious people. It is wholly inadequate to the government of any other."

—John Quincy Adams

Upon his return to France, John Quincy Adams had just turned 12 years of age, and although still quite young, he had already amassed a considerable amount of worldly experience. As soon as the father and son returned, John Quincy was enrolled back into private school and began to once again pour over his studies in Latin and Greek, as well as French.

His father, meanwhile, took on his role as plenipotentiary in earnest. This pursuit would ultimately prove to be one of disillusionment for the elder statesman, however, and Adams would become convinced that the French were stringing the Americans along. Adams early on sought to negotiate a workable peace with Britain to end hostilities and expressed to his French counterparts this desire. He soon concluded that the French had no such wish since it was in France's best interest to let the Americans and British pummel each other into oblivion, while the French Crown sought to retake lost ground in the New World.

John Adams' most immediate disappointment in his efforts came in the form of the French Foreign Minister Count of Vergennes, who was said to counter any suggestion Adams made to promote peace negotiations with objections shrouded in niceties. It was out of his frustrations with the brick wall he had run into in France that Adams began to look toward the nearby Netherlands with a curious eye, wondering if additional aid could be gained from the Dutch.

With this hope in mind, Adams took his son with him to Amsterdam, where John Quincy, despite being merely 13 years old, was accepted into the Dutch University of Leiden. Adams, proud of his son's precociousness, declared in part, "You have now a prize in your hands indeed. If you do not improve to the best advantage, you will be without excuse. But as I know you have an ardent thirst for knowledge and a good capacity to acquire it—you will do no dishonour to yourself nor to the University of Leiden."

John Quincy Adams did not disappoint; he was an excellent student. He especially excelled in French—so much so that other American diplomats began to take notice. One of those diplomats was the American minister to Russia, Francis Dana. John Quincy Adams was just 14 years old when Dana suggested he accompany him to Russia as his interpreter.

It may sound puzzling to modern readers as to why an ambassador to Russia would choose John Quincy, who was fluent only in English and French, as an interpreter. But at this time, French was the common language among nobility, and the Russian royal court were all quite capable of speaking in French. John Quincy's ability to speak flawless French therefore was quite helpful for Dana as he sought to gain Russian recognition of America's independence from Britain.

In the summer of 1781, John Quincy Adams left his lodgings in the Netherlands and disembarked on the 2,000-mile journey from Amsterdam to St. Petersburg. Although he was incredibly young for the role in which he had been placed, John Quincy Adams proved to be a completely able and wholly dedicated member of the American mission to Russia.

John Quincy was quite impressed with the Russian metropolis, writing in his journal at the time, "The city of Petersburg is the finest I ever saw. It is by far superior to Paris, both for the breadth of its streets, and the elegance of the private buildings." The dignitaries of St. Petersburg, however, were not quite so impressed with Dana and young Adams. Rather than receiving the royal welcome from the Queen Catherine of Russia and her court, Dana and Adams' requests for an audience were repeatedly ignored.

While they waited to be heard, summer turned to winter and soon their number one goal was simply to stay warm in the brutal Russian cold. Holed up in their lodgings during the winter months, John Quincy mostly stayed inside reading his books. His father, who was still stationed in the Netherlands, grew increasingly concerned about his son's welfare. He wrote a letter to him during this period that read in part, "I am . . . very uneasy on your account. I want you with me. . . . I want you to pursue your studies at Leiden." As intelligent and independent as his young son was, John Adams was obviously still anxious about how the teenager was getting on. His father's concerns soon won out, and John Quincy decided to return to his dear father in the Netherlands, but only after stopping by Scandinavia and Germany.

Upon their reunion, John Adams was amazed at how much his son had grown both physically and psychologically. He wrote a letter to Abigail back in America around this time, proclaiming, "John is everything you could wish. Wholly devoted to his studies, he has made a progress which gives me entire satisfaction. . . . He is grown a man in understanding and stature as well. . . . I shall take him with me to Paris and shall make much of his company."

John Adams did indeed take his son with him to Paris. By then, the war had turned decidedly in America's favor and negotiations for its cessation were already underway. Standing shoulder to shoulder with the likes of Benjamin Franklin and other revolutionary heroes, John Quincy Adams, now 16 years of age, bore witness to the first official intimations of peace.

Due to his language proficiency, he was soon tasked with editing and transcribing many of the official documents drafted during these talks. John Quincy was right there on the scene, when finally, on September 3, 1783, British minister David Hartley met with John Adams, Benjamin Franklin, and others to officially sign the Treaty of Paris on behalf of Britain, ending all conflict with the duly recognized United States of America.

Chapter Three

Entering the Political Arena

"Whenever vanity and gaiety, a love of pomp and dress, furniture, equipage, buildings, great company, expensive diversions, and elegant entertainments get the better of the principles and judgments of men and women, there is no knowing where they will stop, nor into what evils, natural, moral, or political, they will lead us."

—John Quincy Adams

John Quincy Adams made his long-awaited homecoming back to America in 1785. Shortly after his arrival, he enrolled himself at Harvard where he began to produce routinely high marks in all of his courses. Due to his efforts, he would graduate second in his class in 1787. Immediately after his graduation, the ambitious John Quincy Adams then went on to study law under the guidance of Theophilus Parsons, an esteemed attorney who would one day sit on the Supreme Court.

Under the tutelage of Parsons, John Quincy rapidly educated himself on all of the legal standards of the day. When he wasn't pouring over law books, he was spending time with his friends and writing poetry—the latter of which he had developed such a passion for that at times he even considered giving up the legal practice altogether in order to become a serious poet.

John Quincy's father, meanwhile, had returned from abroad with great fanfare as a notable patriot on par with George Washington and Benjamin Franklin. It was riding in on this popular tide that in April of 1789, when George Washington was elected president, John Adams was given the office of vice president, creating the very first U.S. administration after the Revolutionary War.

John Quincy watched these happenings with pride and a short time later, he finished his bar examinations, ready to strike out on his own. He went into practice as an attorney on August 9, 1790, but despite the fame of his family name, he initially had trouble gaining clients. The first few weeks had John Quincy bored out of his mind waiting long hours for a clientele that simply wasn't forthcoming.

Without any clients to see, he often spent his time reading and writing. His journal entries from this period tell it all. At one point, he jotted down a sarcastic quip, "Very busy with nothing to do." This lack of prospects continued into his first year, and by November, he had only managed to oversee a handful of cases, none of which paid him enough money even to merit his efforts. It was only the benevolence of his father that kept his practice up and running. John Adams would send his son a monthly influx of money to make sure the rent for his law office was paid on time.

His inability to pay his own way in life left John Quincy Adams feeling quite miserable, a sentiment that he keenly expressed in a letter he penned to his older sister Nabby at the time, "I have a profession without employment. The hope of supporting myself is probably somewhat distant." John Adams, for his part, tried to encourage his son, at one point advising him, "It is accident commonly which furnishes the first occasions to a young lawyer to spread his reputation." To make him not feel quite so useless while he awaited such a random opportunity to arrive, John Adams put his son in charge of family finances, granting him power of attorney.

But the only thing that really seemed to encourage John Quincy was when his father had him to come down to Philadelphia—the then capital of the United States—in order to witness the young American government in action. Here, after hobnobbing with the political power brokers of the day, John Quincy was reminded of all his past exploits as a diplomat abroad and felt quite at home.

As such, by the time he returned to his practice in Boston, he felt reinvigorated and with a new purpose in life. Even though hardly anyone would darken his law office door, he had been imbued with a new determination to not just practice law, but to make it. John Quincy Adams was now ready to insert himself wholeheartedly into the political arena.

Chapter Four

Speaking Out Against Thomas Paine

"I speak as a man of the world to men of the world; and I say to you, Search the Scriptures! The Bible is the book of all others, to be read at all ages, and in all conditions of human life; not to be read once or twice or thrice through, and then laid aside, but to be read in small portions of one or two chapters every day, and never to be intermitted unless by some overruling necessity."

—John Quincy Adams

In 1791, John Quincy Adams was finally able to gain enough clients at his law office to support himself and pay his way in life. Even with this modest success, however, he was no longer interested in simply being a lawyer for the rest of his life. He began to turn his attentions to the political intrigue of his day.

France was struggling through the first couple of years of the French Revolution and already in quite a precarious state. Many Americans considered it natural to support the cause of the French Revolution, likening it to America's struggle to free itself from British rule. John Quincy Adams, however, who had been previously immersed in the political and social circles of France, begged to differ.

He knew firsthand how dangerous the French Revolution was in its aims to completely overturn French society and was ready to warn others against invoking such chaos. In this, he took particular issue with the British philosopher Thomas Paine. Although a Brit, Paine was by no means loyal to the British Crown and had instead famously stirred American hearts to the revolutionary cause with his famous pamphlets *Common Sense* and *The American Crisis*, which he had penned during the Revolutionary War.

After the Americans had successfully gained their independence, Paine, the inveterate rabble-rouser, soon turned his attentions to France. After the Treaty of Paris, France had found itself in a rather peculiar position. The French king, in order to antagonize his arch-nemesis of Britain, had sided with the Americans in their efforts to shake off British rule. This was pure pragmatism on his part, however, and King Louis XVI, an absolute monarch, certainly had no interest in democracy or the rights of the individual citizen. His hens would come home to roost in a dramatic fashion, however, when shortly after the Revolutionary War in America came to a conclusion, the French Revolution erupted, forcing the French king from the throne.

In the aftermath, Paine had quickly hightailed it over to France to support the French cause and had soon penned a piece called *Rights of Man*, where he not only supported the French revolutionaries but also called for the overthrow of the British monarchy. Upon hearing this, John Quincy Adams was incensed and felt that the whole idea was absurd. Britain, after all, was a constitutional monarchy.

Even though a king was in place, there was a parliament and the average citizenry had more rights and privileges than most other parts of the world at the time. It may not have been a perfect system, but John Quincy Adams felt that it was certainly better than Thomas Paine's calls to tear it down completely, potentially destabilizing the entire country.

His disgust with Paine's polemics inspired John Quincy Adams to write an open letter for Boston's *Columbian Centinel*. On its printed pages, Adams argued, "His intention appears evidently to be to convince the people of Great Britain that they have neither liberty nor a constitution—that their only possible means to produce these blessings to themselves is to 'topple down headlong' their present government and follow implicitly the example of the French."

John Quincy Adams' warnings against following the "example of the French" would soon prove to be quite prescient as the French Revolution turned into complete chaos, mob violence, and mass executions. Even Thomas Paine would be caught up in what the French later termed "The Terror," and he was arrested and tried by a kangaroo court which had suddenly deemed the former adulator as an enemy agent. In the end, Paine would barely escape being beheaded by the guillotine as the French revolutionary drama continued to unfold.

The writings of John Quincy Adams initially divided the public with some feeling that it was the duty of America to help support the French while others condemned the wanton violence that the French Terror had exacted. As the situation in France continued to grow worse, Adams' supporters soon outweighed his critics, and it was on the power of this new literary fame that John Quincy was viewed as a great political mind in his own right. Doors were opening before him, and before long, the city of Boston enlisted Adams to sit down on the board of citizen committees. Here, he would work to help streamline the practices of the police department and oversee redistricting and local city ordinances.

Impressed by Adams' work and writing, President George Washington began to consider his vice president's son for a role in his administration. So it was, in 1794, that President Washington gave John Quincy Adams the job of U.S. minister to the Netherlands. The Netherlands at the time was on the front lines of French Revolutionary fervor. While stationed here, John Quincy Adams took every opportunity he could to encourage his associates back home to stay out of the war—a task that would prove much easier said than done.

Chapter Five

The Rise of Napoleonic France

"There are three points of doctrine the belief of which forms the foundation of all morality. The first is the existence of God; the second is the immortality of the human soul, and the third is a future state of rewards and punishments. Suppose it possible for a man to disbelieve either of these three articles of faith and that man will have no conscience, he will have no other law than that of the tiger or the shark."

—John Quincy Adams

John Quincy Adams departed for the Netherlands on September 17, 1794; he was 27 years old at the time. Upon his arrival, much of western Europe was in chaos and upheaval thanks to the French Revolution. Just a couple months prior, Maximilien Robespierre, the architect of The Terror, which had summarily executed so many French citizens for any perceived trespass imaginable, was himself beheaded by the guillotine.

After the execution of Robespierre, the French Revolution entered a new phase in which a five-man Directory was established. A leading figure of this Directory was a French general by the name of Napoleon

Bonaparte. Napoleon, seizing upon the desperate state of the French masses, promised all who would follow him riches and glory. He channeled anger, fear, and discontent of the masses when he declared, "Our stores are empty while those of our enemies are overflowing. I will lead you into the most fertile plains in the world. Rich provinces and great cities will be in your power. There you will find honour, glory and wealth."

Napoleon, an experienced general who had already fought in numerous battles, convinced the French that if they could not find a solution to their problems internally, they just might find it externally. As such, an increasingly belligerent France began to spill out of its known borders and into the backyard of the Netherlands where John Quincy Adams was stationed.

While threats from France loomed dark, Adams was sent over to London to join a delegation consisting of Chief Justice John Jay and the U.S. ambassador to England, Thomas Pinckney. This mission, which would help to charter the state of post-war relations between Britain and the United States, became known as the Jay Treaty.

As consequential as this treaty was for the future of the United States, Adams' visit to England proved rather significant for his personal life as well. For it was here that John Quincy Adams met his soon-to-be wife, Louisa Catherine Johnson. Although Louisa had been born in England, she was actually the daughter of an American diplomat. Adams hoped that these American ties would be enough to persuade his parents of the match, but they still had their reservations, knowing that much of the American public was quite suspicious of anything to do with Britain.

John Quincy was eventually able to assuage the fears and concerns of his parents, and he and Louisa were duly wed in the summer of 1797.

Louisa's father meanwhile had run afoul of business associates in Britain and had fled the country. This left Adams bereft of the dowry that he had been promised. Not only that, but some of the creditors even attempted to go after John Quincy Adams in his father-in law's absence. Dowry or not, however, Adams stood by his bride and attempted to soothe her pain and humiliation that this family discord had brought.

His own father, meanwhile, had won the 1796 presidential election, becoming the second U.S. president to be inaugurated into office in 1797. Despite some accusing the newly elected John Adams of engaging in nepotism, he decided that he would keep his son as ambassador. John Quincy's next mission field was at the royal court of Prussia.

It is worth noting that Prussia, of course, is a country that no longer exists. Prior to Berlin being the capital of Germany, it was the capital of Prussia. John Quincy Adam's major accomplishment during his tenure in the Prussian capital was to negotiate a trade agreement on behalf of the United States, but perhaps his most memorable work during this period was the prodigious correspondence he carried out on the subject of Prussia's Silesian countryside, which would later become the contents of a book named *Letters on Silesia*. While John Quincy was enjoying the sights in the countryside, however, Europe was once again receiving ominous tidings from France.

By the time of his return to Berlin, Prussia was all abuzz with the news that the French had a new head of state in the form of one Napoleon Bonaparte. General Bonaparte had just barely escaped from the jaws of defeat after a failed expedition in Egypt, yet upon his return to Paris he was more popular than ever before. With the help of his supporters, Napoleon was able to stage a complete takeover of the French government.

Although Napoleon would soon bring much devastation to Europe, initially the change in leadership seemed quite good for America. Just prior to Napoleon, the French had been antagonizing American shipping, seizing craft and imprisoning crew. Napoleon realized that it made no sense to make an enemy out of America and quickly sought to normalize relations, resulting in a peace treaty signed on September 30, 1800.

Despite the fact that this allowed President Adams to retain the neutrality that George Washington himself had championed, Adams failed to win re-election that November and was bested by his opponent and soon-to-be third president of the U.S., Thomas Jefferson. With his father being recalled from the White House, John Quincy Adams was recalled from his Prussian post as well.

Chapter Six

Work in the Senate

"Let us not be unmindful that liberty is power, that the nation blessed with the largest portion of liberty must in proportion to its numbers be the most powerful nation upon Earth. Our Constitution professedly rests upon the good sense and attachment of the people. This basis, weak as it may appear, has not yet been found to fail. Always vote for a principle, though you vote alone, and you may cherish the sweet reflection that your vote is never lost. America, in the assembly of nations, has uniformly spoken among them the language of equal liberty, equal justice, and equal rights."

—John Quincy Adams

Just a few weeks prior to his receiving his marching orders to head back to the United States, John Quincy Adams and his wife Louisa had welcomed their first child into the world. The baby boy, who they named George Washington Adams, was born on April 12, 1801. Just a few months later, on June 17, Adams' now family of three boarded a clipper ship and set sail for America.

The family established itself in Boston where John Quincy once again opened a law office. As was the case previously, he quickly bored of his work as an attorney and began to dabble in local politics, becoming involved with local committees, clubs, and organizations—all of which culminated in his election to the State Senate in the spring of 1802.

During his tenure in the State Senate, Adams initially positioned himself as a reformer who would fight corruption. He soon found that these altruistic efforts would bring the wrath of both the Federalist and Republican parties down upon him. Having enough of his meddling, the State legislature actually gave John Quincy a promotion, sending him to the U.S. Senate and that way relocating the troublesome senator out of Massachusetts to the recently established Washington, D.C. They figured this would put an end to his interference, but little did they know that John Quincy Adams was just getting started.

Before the family headed out to Washington, Louisa successfully gave birth to the couple's second child on July 4, 1803, who was named John Adams II after his grandfather who came before. A few months later, once the growing family had settled into their new life in Washington, John Quincy got to work in the Senate. One of the first major issues that he presided over in the Senate was in regard to the Louisiana Purchase.

Happenings in Revolutionary France were once again affecting U.S. interest, this time in the form of a bargain being struck by the French dictator Napoleon Bonaparte. Napoleon, weary under the strain of constant war abroad and dwindling resources at home, had decided to give up French holdings in Louisiana territory in exchange for 15 million dollars. To be sure, 15 million was a lot of money back then, but it was nowhere near the return of investment that the U.S. would receive from the purchase. The Louisiana territory comprised no less than a million square miles of the westward expanse of the North American continent. This resource rich land would quickly pay back every cent spent to acquire it.

The most consequential issue to arise during Adams' first term in the Senate, however, was over the impeachment of an associate justice of the Supreme Court by the name of Samuel Chase, who was being run out of office on the grounds that he was too partisan. The justice had apparently made some rather bias statements in the past, and the House of Representatives wished to hold him to account. They charged that by way of his biased, impartial remarks, the justice had committed "high crimes and misdemeanours" including sedition and treason, two impeachable offenses according to the constitution. John Quincy Adams immediately voiced his oppositions to the measures.

To be clear, it wasn't that Adams agreed with the justice's remarks, but he did not believe that they rose to the level of an impeachable offense. Adams maintained that when the founders used the phrase "high crimes and misdemeanours," they did so in reference to clear criminal intent and not just mere, offhand, politically charged statements. Most of his colleagues agreed, with the Senate voting to acquit the impeached chief justice on March 1, 1805. For Quincy, this was not a victory for Samuel Chase so much as it was a victory for free speech, or as he called it, the prevention of the House of Representatives from criminalizing the first amendment that allowed that said free speech in the first place.

In reflection of the trial that had taken place, John Quincy Adams felt proud of his role in the process, which he declared, "exhibited the Senate of the United States fulfilling the most important purpose of its institution, by putting a check upon the impetuous violence of the House of Representatives. It has proved that a sense of justice is yet strong enough to overpower the furies of faction." John Quincy Adams stood up for what he believed in, defended the Constitution, and emerged victorious.

Chapter Seven

The Unpopular Embargo Act

"America does not go abroad in search of monsters to destroy. She is the well-wisher to the freedom and independence of all. She well knows that by enlisting under other banners than her own, were they even the banners of foreign independence, she would involve herself beyond the power of extrication in all the wars of interest and intrigue, of individual avarice, envy, and ambition, which assume the colors and the standards of freedom."

—John Quincy Adams

By the year 1807, John Quincy Adams had reached a decided crossroads during his tenure in the Senate. The previous year had seen a renewed spate of hostilities emanating from France, and as the war between Britain and France in particular heated up, the British determined that American shipping in French waters were forfeit.

Making matters worse, American shipping had come under assault by the British just a few nautical miles from American soil. On June 22, 1807, a British warship seized an American craft called the *Chesapeake* on the pretense that they were searching for a few British troops that had recently gone AWOL. Whatever the case may be, once the

British boarded the American craft, the results were brutal. One man was executed on the spot while three others were taken back to the British craft as prisoners.

The United States had long attempted to maintain a neutral footing and, still not wishing to take a side in the conflict, it was determined that perhaps shutting out all actors in the crisis would be the next best thing. So it was that Congress came up with the so-called Embargo Act of 1807. This act essentially enacted a wholesale embargo of all European nations. It was believed that once all supplies from America were shut off, both Britain and France would be forced to cease their belligerence and come to terms. Yet with such an impediment placed upon U.S. trade, it doesn't take much to imagine the toll that this sweeping measure would take on the American economy.

Nonetheless, John Quincy Adams viewed it as the only viable option that the United States had for leverage. He knew that America was in no shape for an all-out military confrontation, and yet allowing U.S. shipping to continue to be confiscated by foreign powers was inconceivable as well. In John Quincy's mind, the punitive measures on trade that the Embargo Act of 1807 espoused was the best option they had. As the nation entered into this bargain, Louisa meanwhile gave birth to what would be their third child, Charles Francis, whom John Quincy had named after his own brother Charles, who had passed away some years before.

While it was a joyful time for the Adams family, it wasn't long before the political winds began to shift against John Quincy, and he found himself on some rather perilous grounds. By shutting down America's ports completely, the

Embargo Act ended up hurting the United States much more than it did Britain. Quincy and his cohorts believed that the United States could temporarily refrain from exporting and importing goods in favor of homegrown industry, but the surplus goods ended up just sitting on the docks and the effect on the economy was rather dire as a result.

It was his association with this failed policy that all but sealed Adams' fate in the next election cycle. Adams failed to get re-elected to the Senate and ended up resigning before the end of his remaining term. It seemed to be a bitter end to what had otherwise been a promising political career.

Chapter Eight

Rise to the Top

"Individual liberty is individual power, and as the power of a community is a mass compounded of individual powers, the nation which enjoys the most freedom must necessarily be in proportion to its numbers the most powerful nation."

—John Quincy Adams

Upon the ringing in of the New Year in 1808, John Quincy Adams was in no mood to celebrate. His political aspirations had been dashed, and his outlook toward his future prospects were decidedly bleak. Even when some of his associates suggested that he could ditch the Federalists who had abandoned him and run as a Republican instead, Adams refused. He felt that his political career had come to an end, and the only thing left for him to do was to retreat to private life. As such, he went back to his legal practice in Boston and began to once again see clients as a run of the mill lawyer. But nevertheless, someone of John Quincy Adams' stature, a former senator, the son of a former president, and an inveterate expert on foreign affairs, would not be able to stay out of the political fray for long.

In 1809, Adams was appointed to take on the post of U.S. minister to Russia for the incoming administration of President James Madison. Although ostensibly happy that their son's talents were being made use of, it is said that both John and Abigail Adams couldn't help but be sad that John Quincy was once again being sent abroad. They were both getting older and feared that they might perish before seeing their son again.

Nevertheless, on August 5, 1809, John Quincy Adams set sail for Russia as planned, bringing with him his wife and youngest son. They made landfall in St. Petersburg late that fall. Tsar Alexander I, a ruler positioned to be a reformer, had recently risen to the throne and it was a time of great change for Russia. For John Quincy Adams, the main bulk of his work consisted of giving an ear to Russian diplomats while gathering as much valuable intel as he could for the State Department back home. Here, John Quincy Adams fell right back into court life, with most of his days consisting of dinners and dances in which he hobnobbed with the Russian elite.

Their time in the Russian capital would be forever marred, however, by the abrupt passing of their new baby daughter, Louisa Catherine. The loss hit Adams hard. He noted the tragedy in a journal entry dated for September 15, 1812, with a poignant account which stated, "At twenty-five minutes past one this morning, expired my daughter Louisa Catherine, as lovely an infant as ever breathed the air of heaven."

After the death of his child, John Quincy Adams quietly buried himself in his work, becoming quite close to Alexander I. From his perch, he had bore witness to the Russians successfully beating back the French in 1811. In 1812, however, a new ominous note in the conflict was sounded not from Napoleonic France but from Britain, as the War of 1812 began to take shape. Adams viewed this as an unmitigated disaster, and with the help of the Russian tsar he sought to create an American delegation based in St. Petersburg that would be able to negotiate an end to the conflict. The British refused to show up at these peace talks, and instead negotiations would drag on until 1814 when Adams and his delegation finally met up with their British counterparts in Ghent, Belgium to sign the Treaty of Ghent, finally ending the war.

Many lives had been lost, and much property had been destroyed in the process, but Adams was satisfied that peace with the British finally seemed possible. President Madison had been quite impressed with John Quincy's efforts and decided to appoint him as the official U.S. ambassador to the British. During his tenure, he managed to secure a limited trade agreement with Britain, but the vast majority of his time was occupied by his efforts of repatriating American prisoners of war back to the United States.

Shortly thereafter, the presidency changed hands with the election of James Monroe. Monroe, like Madison, viewed John Quincy Adams with high regard—so much so that he chose Quincy for the role of secretary of state in 1817. John Quincy Adams would remain in this role for the duration of Monroe's two terms in office, a tenure spanning from 1817 to 1825. During most of his time as secretary of state, John Quincy Adams' primary focus was continuing to avoid major conflict with European powers abroad and consolidating American resources at home.

One European power that seemed ripe for American aggression, however, was that of Spain. Spain, the first European country to even lay claim to the New World, had long been in decline. Now the Spanish territories of Florida and the American southwest seemed ripe for plunder, with many wishing to expand America's reach as Spain began to lose its grip on its colonial territory. Of the territories slipping out of Spain's hands, Florida was the most precarious.

Exhausted by its efforts during the Napoleonic Wars, Spain could no longer provide adequate troop support in Florida which had since become practically overrun by a local Native American tribal group, the Seminoles. It was under this duress that Spain agreed to cede Florida to the United States in the Adams-Onis Treaty. Similar to the Louisiana Purchase, for the cost of just five million dollars, Florida was made a part of the United States.

Riding high on these accomplishments, Monroe's second term came to a close, and he designated John Quincy Adams as his successor. With the 1824 presidential election looming before him, now like his father, John Quincy Adams would seek the highest office in the land.

Chapter Nine

Adams as President

"I am a warrior, so that my son may be a merchant, so that his son may be a poet."

—John Quincy Adams

During the presidential election of 1824, many were under the impression that a John Quincy Adams' candidacy would be a sure thing. If anyone had an experienced resume for the job of president, Adams most certainly did. He was the son of a president, a lifelong diplomat, and a former senator and secretary of state. Nevertheless, he faced an unexpectedly strong challenger in the form of the War of 1812 hero, General Andrew Jackson.

Andrew Jackson was what we would term today as a populist and had tremendous appeal to the average American. His charm was indeed nearly enough to defeat John Quincy Adams in the 1824 election, but in the end, John Quincy Adams prevailed and was inaugurated as the sixth president of the United States.

During his time in office, John Quincy Adams would continue to pursue his two-pronged approach of peace abroad, while strengthening America at home. In this, one of his first major efforts as president was to engage in massive building projects for new roads and rail lines. To match his ambition, Adams created the Department of the

Interior. President Adams, through this means, desired to bring the scattered corners of the union together, with a more reliable means of transport across the interior of America. Most would have welcomed these efforts, but there were those in the opposition party who were worried that Quincy's was engaged in an overreach of power, putting way too much emphasis on overarching federal directive rather than allowing the states to contribute their own input on the matter.

Despite his critics, Adams was able to glean enough support to go forward with his major overhaul of infrastructure, creating new highways, railways, and byways all over the land. Adams hoped that these efforts to improve the lives of the average citizen would gain him enough goodwill to secure a second term in office. But by the time of the midpoint of his presidency, conflict began to arise once again. Citing Manifest Destiny, many wished for a more aggressive expansion into the western territories which were primarily occupied by Native American groups. Adams, not wishing to rock the boat, called for a much more cautious approach and wished to gradually integrate the Native American populations of the west as fellow members of the United States.

John Quincy Adams was an altruistic soul, ahead of his time, and his sentiments on this matter proved it. While many others wouldn't give a second thought about displacing Native Americans, Adams sought to ease them into American life as painlessly as possible. Sadly, this approach would ultimately cost John Quincy Adams re-election, as the public clamored for a man who had no qualms with displacing Native Americans—his recent political rival, General Andrew Jackson.

In fact, after his defeat by Adams in 1824, Andrew Jackson had never really stopped campaigning. By the midterms, he was already actively getting ready for his second run with his avid supporters, so-called Jacksonians, making presidential life for John Quincy Adams difficult every step of the way. Adding to his misery was the passing of his father, John Adams, on July 4, 1826. The elder American statesmen passed away on the day which served to commemorate the Declaration of Independence which had occurred some 50 years prior. Too many, it may have seemed like a fitting end, but for John Quincy Adams it was simply a sad ending to one of the most important chapters of his life. Despite his sadness, however, his upcoming bid for re-election would soon consume his thoughts.

In many ways, John Quincy Adams and Andrew Jackson were opposites. John Quincy Adams was a cerebral intellectual whereas Andrew Jackson was a military man who spoke from his gut. While John Quincy Adams had the full potential of alienating an audience by speaking to them like a college professor, Andrew Jackson knew precisely how to rile up his base. Jackson was also good at attacking his opponents. It was perhaps Jackson's razor tongue that the Adams campaign feared the most as they geared up for the 1828 presidential election. For this reason, Adams' associates sought to pre-empt Jackson by levelling blistering attacks of their own.

In their efforts, Adams' team managed to procure some rather salacious—at least by nineteenth-century standards—material on Jackson. It was discovered that when Jackson first met his wife, she was not yet divorced from her previous husband. Adams' supporters began to trumpet this inuendo in the press to make it seem as if Jackson had married out of an adulterous affair. Jackson and company immediately returned fire, however, and began to attack John Quincy Adams' wife Louise, labelling her as an aristocratic, English wife due to the fact that she grew up in Britain.

Yet it wasn't the smear campaigns that decided the 1828 election; it was simply the sheer contrast between the two characters involved. John Quincy Adams was seen as out of touch and disconnected from the American people, whereas Andrew Jackson seemed to have his fingers right on the average citizen's pulse. In the end, Jackson's rough and tumble brand of populism simply won out against John Quincy Adams' more urbane intellectual discourse. When the election results came in, they reflected this fact with Jackson winning 178 votes in the electoral college compared to John Quincy Adams' mere 83. Jackson also won the popular vote by a wide margin, making it a landslide victory for the old general.

John Quincy was deeply disappointed by the results, but at the same time accepted his fate. A journal entry he made at the time seemed to sum up these complicated feelings best when he wrote, "The sun of my political life sets in the deepest gloom but that of my country shines unclouded."

Chapter Ten

Late Life and Death

"Find a mission that you can give yourself over to and then spend your days moving that mission forward. Man is made so that when anything fires his soul the impossibilities vanish. The influence of each human being on others in this life is a kind of immortality."

—John Quincy Adams

The aftermath of the 1828 presidential election was a bitter pill for John Quincy Adams to swallow, but there was more than enough bitterness to go around. Andrew Jackson, although the victor of this match, retained considerable rancor and animosity toward John Quincy Adams and even blamed him for his wife's death. Jackson's wife Rachel, who was so mercilessly targeted during the campaign, died of a heart attack shortly after Jackson won the election. Andrew Jackson believed that it was the strain of the attacks against her character that had killed her, and he would forever hold it against John Quincy Adams and his supporters.

Adams, for his part, feeling roundly rejected by the American electorate, decided to hole up at his deceased father's estate where he proceeded to write his biography and occasionally offer his legal services to the locals. It wasn't long into this semi-retirement that John Quincy

Adams received the terrible news that his oldest son, 28-year-old George Washington Adams, had died. His son had apparently fallen off or jumped off the deck of a steamboat after a night of heavy drinking and drowned.

It was a rather inglorious end for a former president's son and only added to John Quincy Adams' misery and woe. In the midst of this trauma, he tried his best to put his energy into other pursuits. He spent his days reading, writing, taking long walks, and even planting some crops on the estate, but all to no avail. Nothing could satisfy him. It was only when his associates encouraged him to take part in the 1830 midterm elections that John Quincy was able to turn his mind away from his inner turmoil and back to national politics. Some associates of his back in Boston had tipped him off that a local congressman was getting ready to retire from his district and expressed their belief that Adams had a good chance of winning the seat were he to run.

They were right. Once he was finally convinced to make a go of it, John Quincy Adams won his congressional seat by a landslide margin of 1,817 votes compared to the joint sum of the 552 votes held by his two opponents. John Quincy Adams would continue to serve in this capacity from 1831 until his death in 1848.

Even back then, it was highly unusual for a former president to return to public life, and there was quite an element of surprise in Washington, D.C. at the sight of John Quincy Adams' return. No one was more surprised than the then president, Andrew Jackson. Jackson viewed Adams as nothing short of a recurring thorn in his side. All of Washington at this point had become polarized into two separate camps, with one being pro-Jackson and the other being dead set against Jackson. It's not hard to imagine to which side President Jackson's old antagonist John Quincy Adams belonged.

These two factions were more than ever set against each other when one of the biggest dramas of the Jackson presidency, the so-called Nullification Crisis, came to pass in 1832. The basis of the crisis was over South Carolina's rejection of certain federal tariffs which had been enacted in 1828 and 1832. Leaders of South Carolina refused to recognize the tariffs, thereby making them null and void.

The real crisis began when the federals attempted to enforce the rulings and were met with armed resistance from South Carolina's militias. This was too much even for states' rights champion Andrew Jackson to handle, and he began to prepare for the use of military force. Fortunately enough, a new bit of legislation called the Compromise Tariff of 1833 managed to diffuse the volatile situation with both sides backing down.

A few years later, a new president was elected to office by the name of Martin Van Buren. The biggest political issue during this time revolved around the newly independent state of Texas. Texas had just broken away from Mexico and created its own independent republic. Most of the settlers of the Republic of Texas were expatriates from the United States, so it made sense to ultimately seek to bring Texas into the union. Still, there were a few reasons to resist this notion. For one thing, there were those who felt it unwise to antagonize the Spanish by taking on territory they had just lost. Even more contentious than this was the fact that Texas was a slave state.

Since the Declaration of Independence, the balance of the union had rested upon the precarious status of whether a state was free—as in free of slavery—or one that allowed the procurement of slaves. The free northern states did not wish for a large slave espousing state such as Texas to join ranks with the rest of the slaveholding south, fearing that it would upset this delicate balance. Southerners, meanwhile, knowing that such a merger would grant them more representation and therefore more political power, were ceaselessly clamouring for Texas to be accepted into the fold.

John Quincy Adams, who had long been fiercely against slavery, feared that admission of Texas would only widen the scope of the horrid practice. For his part, President Van Buren was concerned that the tensions between the slave states and the free states might lead to all-out aggression and a breakdown of the union. Ultimately, he decided not to pursue the acquisition of Texas during his tenure. Van Buren's successor, John Tyler, would have no such qualms.

Tyler was actually the vice president of the man who defeated Van Buren in the 1840 presidential election, William Henry Harrison. Harrison's time in office would prove incredibly short, however, with him passing away just a few months after being elected. With John Tyler's assumption of the presidency, the acquisition of Texas had once again become a major point of discussion. In 1844, Tyler would go on to seek ratification for an annexation treaty, but it was thrown out by the Senate, putting a halt to

Tyler's efforts. Tyler was meanwhile up for re-election and ended up losing to James K. Polk.

Nevertheless, in his last few months as president, Tyler attempted to pass yet another treaty for the annexation of Texas. Adams immediately went on the offensive, declaring that the treaty would launch America into nothing short of a "war for slavery." Despite his efforts, in 1845, the treaty was finally ratified and Texas was accepted into the union. Shortly thereafter, the United States would become embroiled in a war with Mexico—hostilities that the prescient John Quincy Adams completely opposed.

Even after the war had come to a conclusion, he was bitterly against it, as was demonstrated on February 21, 1848 during a session of Congress when he voted no on the mere suggestion of a measure to honor the generals of the Mexican-American War. After the rest of the members had sounded a union "aye" to the suggestion, John Quincy Adams stood up alone and shouted, "No!" Incredibly enough, it would be the last word he would ever speak before Congress, since seconds later he fell to the ground in a heap, an apparent victim of a stroke.

Conclusion

John Quincy Adams loved his time spent serving in the House of Representatives; in many ways he cherished the wrangling of Congress much more than he ever could the role of president. Having that said, it seems rather fitting that he spent his very last ounce of energy and strength debating with his colleagues in the House.

At the time of his stroke, Adams had collapsed right into the arms of one of his colleagues who was standing nearby. As his body horribly convulsed before them, Adams was quickly led to a couch, where he was laid out as comfortably as his shocked associates could muster. Fellow congressman then picked up the couch and carried Adams out into the rotunda, hoping that the fresher air might revive him. All Adams could do was offer a quiet thanks to those around him, before uttering his last words, "This is the end of Earth, but I am composed." After this, Adams went into a deep sleep from which no one could summon him. He then passed away a couple of days later on February 23, 1848. He was 80 years old.

No matter where they stood on the political aisle, both his friends and foes alike had to admit, that John Quincy Adams' was a life of service until the very end.